To the many natural history museums who have kept my love of dinosaurs from becoming extinct. And a special thanks to Godzilla.

Copyright © 2001 by Bob Barner.
All rights reserved.

Book design by Catherine Jacobes Design, San Francisco.
Typeset in Jaft and Frutiger.
The illustrations in this book were rendered with pen and ink,
watercolor, cut and torn paper and a computer.
Printed in China.

Library of Congress Cataloging-in-Publication Data
Barner, Bob.
    Dinosaur bones / by Bob Barner.
    p. cm.
    ISBN 0-8118-3158-2
    1. Dinosaurs—Juvenile literature. [1. Dinosaurs. 2. Fossils.
        3. Paleontology.] I. Title.
QE861.5 .B36 2001
567.9—1dc21
00-011496

Distributed in Canada by Raincoast Books
9050 Shaughnessy Street
Vancouver, British Columbia V6P 6E5

10 9 8 7 6 5 4 3 2 1

Chronicle Books LLC
85 Second Street
San Francisco, California 94105

www.chroniclebooks.com/Kids

Dinosaur Bones

Bob Barner

chronicle books · san francisco

Dinosaurs are

The last dinosaurs lived 65 million years ago. Dinosaurs became extinct because climate changes made it hard for them to find enough food.

gone for good.

Maybe dinosaurs once lived

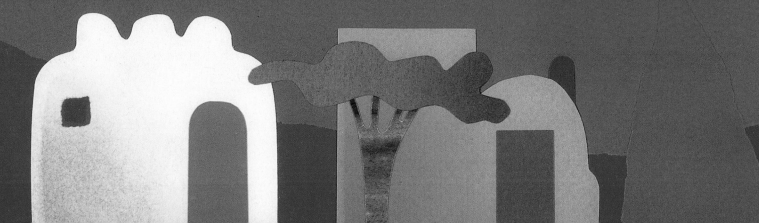

The first dinosaur bones were discovered in England in the 1820's. Since then dinosaur fossils have been found all over the world.

in your neighborhood!

Fossils are bones
and footprints that
have been preserved
in the earth's crust.

Dinosaurs had teeth to bite and jaws to chew.

The shape of the jaws and teeth help scientists find out if a dinosaur was a meat or plant eater. Dinosaurs with sharp teeth like this T. Rex were meat eaters.

They walked the earth

when those bones were new.

Tyranosaurus Rex means "king of tyrant lizards." Its arms were so short it couldn't even scratch its chin. The first T. Rex skeleton was found in Montana in 1902. A T. Rex skull can weigh up to 750 pounds!

They had bones for legs

Scientists study the bones to find out more about dinosaurs. Some dinosaurs had hips like birds. Others had hips like lizards. Many dinosaurs were giants, but some were the size of a chicken.

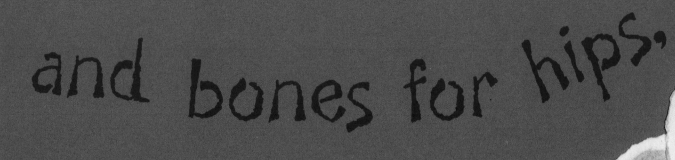

and bones for hips,

dinosaur bones used on

long dinosaur trips.

Some dinosaurs traveled and hunted in groups or herds.
Living in groups helped protect them from predators.
Ancient footprints show that baby dinosaurs were often
protected from predators by walking in the center of
the herd.

They had bones with disks

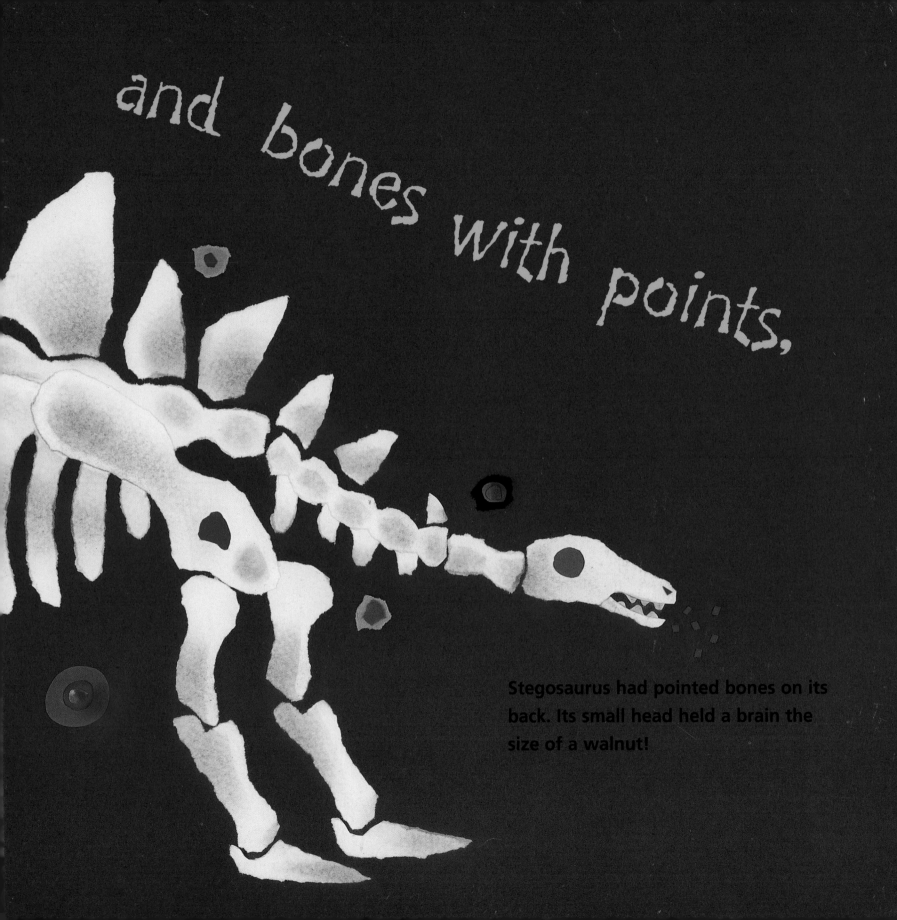

and bones with points,

Stegosaurus had pointed bones on its back. Its small head held a brain the size of a walnut!

bones for running

Stegosaurus spent most of the time munching plants to feed its huge body. It used the spikes on its tail to fight attacks from meat-eating dinosaurs like T. Rex.

with sockets and joints.

are left to show.

Triceratops had a skull one-third
the length of its body. It gathered
plants with its turtle-like beak and
chewed food with teeth in the
back of its mouth.

But dinosaurs rumbled and

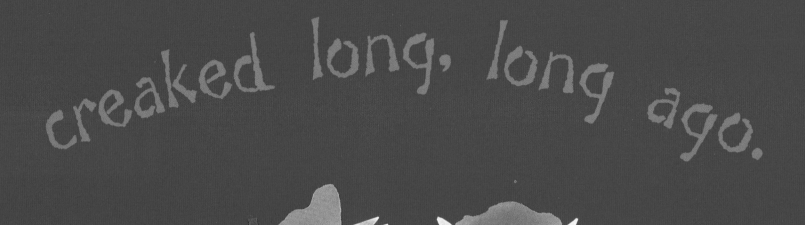

creaked long, long ago.

Triceratops means "three-horned face." This plant eater was generally peaceful. However, it used its long horns to fight when attacked. Triceratops was one of the last dinosaurs to exist.

So, when you see dinosaur bones

Scientists put together dinosaur bones like
a puzzle. They use chisels, diamond saws and
dental drills to remove the bones from rock.
The skeletons are held together with metal
wire and pipes.

at a museum in town,

Brachiosaurus weighed more than ten elephants. It was one of the heaviest and longest dinosaurs. A hungry Brachiosaurus used its long neck to reach tender leaves at the tops of trees.

used them to get around!

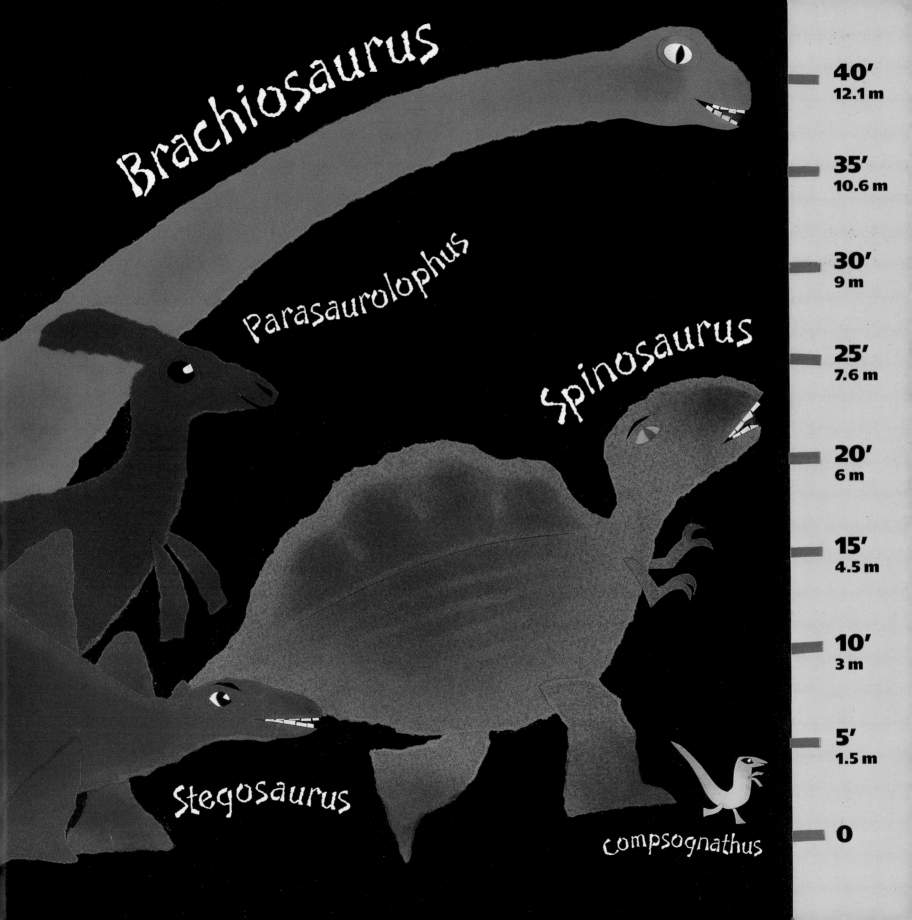

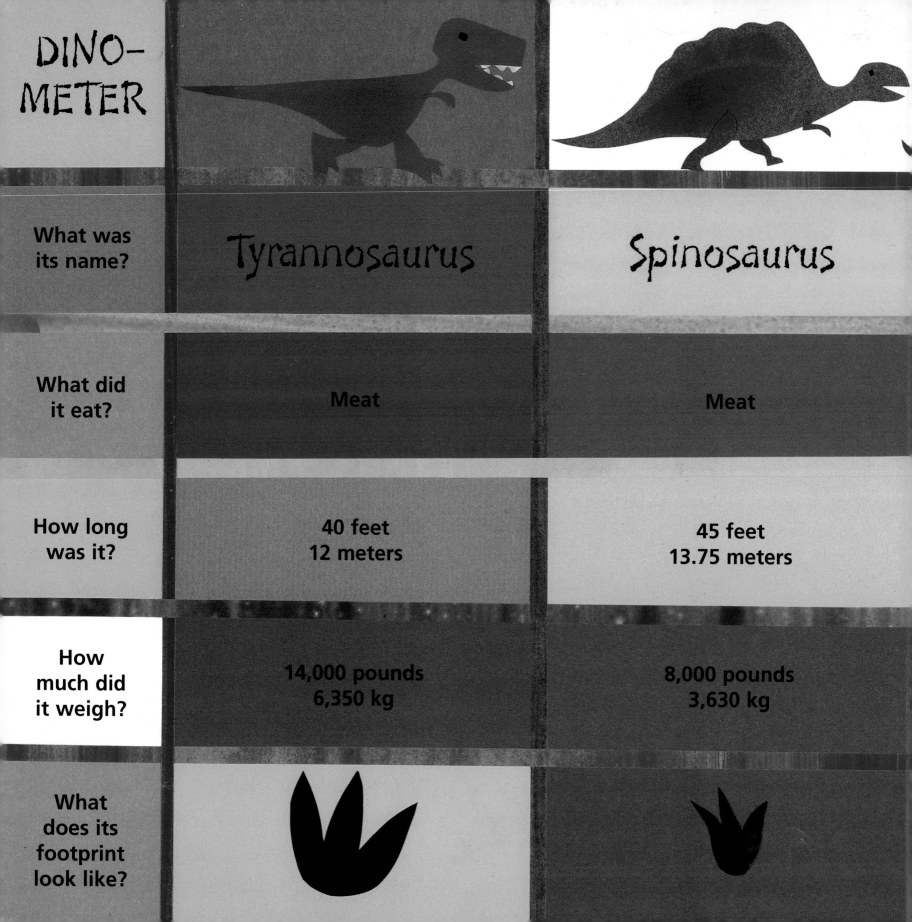

DINO-METER

	Tyrannosaurus	Spinosaurus
What was its name?	Tyrannosaurus	Spinosaurus
What did it eat?	Meat	Meat
How long was it?	40 feet 12 meters	45 feet 13.75 meters
How much did it weigh?	14,000 pounds 6,350 kg	8,000 pounds 3,630 kg
What does its footprint look like?		

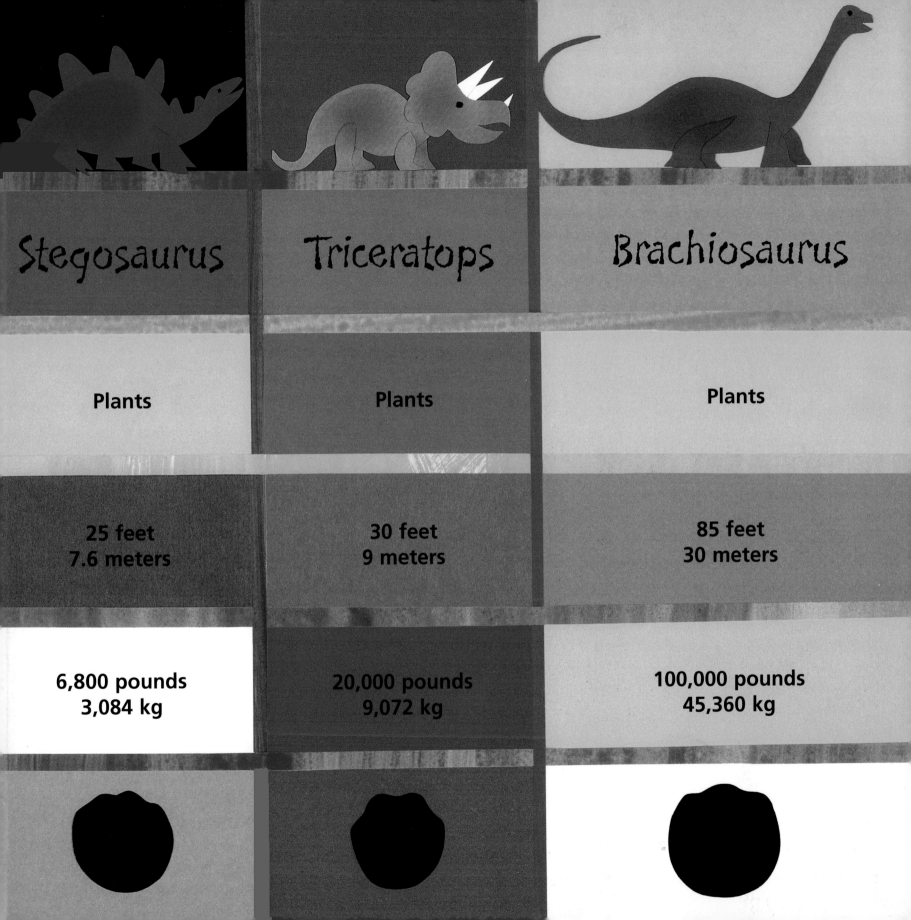

Stegosaurus	Triceratops	Brachiosaurus
Plants	Plants	Plants
25 feet 7.6 meters	30 feet 9 meters	85 feet 30 meters
6,800 pounds 3,084 kg	20,000 pounds 9,072 kg	100,000 pounds 45,360 kg